Dinosaur
BUILDER

Rob Waring, *Series Editor*

NATIONAL
GEOGRAPHIC
LEARNING

Australia · Brazil · Mexico · Singapore · United Kingdom

T0052108

Words to Know

This story is set in Canada.
It takes place near Niagara Falls
in the province of Ontario
[ɒntɛəriou].

 Dinosaurs. Read the paragraph. Then write the basic form of each underlined word next to the correct definition.

Dinosaurs dominated the earth for over 160 million years. Some of these amazing reptiles were quite small, while others were absolutely enormous. Because they are now extinct, much of what scientists know about these animals that roamed our planet so long ago comes from the study of fossils and ancient dinosaur skeletons found underground.

1. the remains of ancient animal or plant life preserved in rock: _____

2. a type of animal that lived millions of years ago: _____

3. wander; move around freely: _____

4. a body's bones: _____

5. no longer in existence: _____

6. a group of cold-blooded animals that have backbones, live on land, and usually produce young by laying eggs: _____

Ancient Fossils

B **Building Dinosaurs.** Read the paragraph. Then match each word with the correct definition.

Peter May's job is to recreate dinosaurs for museum displays. His workshop is full of artificial dinosaur skeletons that will someday be mounted in museums around the world. In order to make them, Peter and his team of craftsmen and women first examine the work of paleontologists to learn about the animal they're going to make. Then, they make casts of the real bones in order to create artificial ones. The artificial bones are made of fiberglass to ensure that they are both strong and light weight.

1. recreate _____

2. workshop _____

3. mount _____

4. craftsman/ woman _____

5. paleontologist _____

6. cast _____

7. fiberglass _____

a. a skilled person, especially one who makes beautiful items by hand
b. a strong, light material made from glass and plastic
c. a building or area with machinery and tools
d. a scientist who studies fossils and bones
e. put on display; hang up
f. make something from the past exist again
g. an object made by pouring hot liquid into a container and cooling it to copy a specific shape

A Dinosaur Skeleton

Even before the days of Hollywood's big hit dinosaur movies, museum dinosaur displays have long been something that fascinated children and adults alike. These mysterious reptiles that roamed the earth millions of years ago have kept people's interest for years. The enormous skeletons of dinosaurs seen in museums often fill viewers with amazement and wonder as they wander through the huge halls. However, few people likely consider who makes these incredible creations, and more importantly how. Constructing these fascinating museum displays is actually a unique combination of art, **craft**,[1] and science, and it requires a combination of skills that very few have mastered.

Perhaps the top dinosaur builder in the world is a Canadian craftsman named Peter May. It's his job to reconstruct the huge dinosaur skeletons found by paleontologists and he does it in his workshop not far from Niagara Falls, Ontario. Here, May creates these amazing reminders of life on our Earth millions of years ago and sends them to museums all around the world. Obviously, it's not a quiet art studio filled will paper and paints; it's a huge open room full of machines and various types of equipment needed to make these amazing creations. It also houses several half-finished dinosaur skeletons as well. For some, May's busy workshop may seem a bit like a 'dinosaur construction site' with a diverse collection of ancient beasts in the process of being brought back to life.

---

[1]**craft:** a job or activity requiring skill or experience in making things

 CD 2, Track 01

plate

A dinosaur builder in May's workshop works on a stegosaurus skeleton.

The workshop bursts with noise and activity—and parts of dinosaurs. They hang from the ceiling, sit on large tables, and are transported around the huge facility by large pieces of construction equipment. There are backbones as long as buses, legs as tall as small trees, and heads almost as big as cars. Above them all, one can find terrifying half-finished flying creatures from the distant past hanging in the air, almost as if ready to come to life.

In one corner there's a semi-complete skeleton of a dinosaur that's almost as big as a house. As he stands near the tail of the huge prehistoric beast, May describes the piece. "It's a work in progress on a stegosaurus," he explains, placing his hand gently on the giant skeleton, "and we haven't put the **plates**[2] on it yet or reconstructed the backbone." He then talks about the complexity level of the project adding, "This one is pretty **straightforward**.[3] It's your old standard dinosaur."

Recreating a stegosaurus may be a straightforward task if you're Peter May—but that's because he's one of the world's best at this craft. Most people would find building a dinosaur an extremely difficult assignment, and very few would have the chance to attempt it at all. May explains that even his introduction into the job was a bit arbitrary; he didn't exactly plan to have a career building dinosaurs. "This came right **out of the blue**,"[4] he laughs. "It's just grown. I don't think anybody could sit down in their late teens and say 'I'm going to be a dinosaur builder.'"

---

[2] **plate:** a flat sheet of hard material; in this case the vertical body parts that protected the backbone of the stegosaurus
[3] **straightforward:** clear, direct; without complications
[4] **out of the blue:** *(expression)* occurring randomly with no warning

The story of how Peter May became a dinosaur builder is an interesting topic, one which actually grew out of staff problems at the world's museums. May began his career working at Toronto's Royal Ontario Museum in the early 1980s. Later, however, many of the museums around the globe could no longer afford to keep experts like May on their staff since they often only need a new display every few decades. This is how the Canadian dinosaur builder found the job that seemed suited for him. Instead of limiting himself to one museum that wouldn't always need his help putting up new displays, he started hiring himself out as a **freelancer**.[5] That way any museum in the world could contract him to mount a display when they needed him rather than employ a full-time dinosaur builder. Before long, May became very busy.

Kevin Seymour of the Royal Ontario Museum explains how May does it. "So, he found that if he freelanced, then the museums of the world could come to him when they needed him," he says. "And that's what's happening. He has jobs in Europe and in Japan and all around the world." Seymour adds, "Most people believe he's the best." Looking at the amount of work in his workshop, being the best has obviously helped May's business.

---

[5]**freelancer:** someone who works as an independent, self-employed person performing jobs for a variety of companies

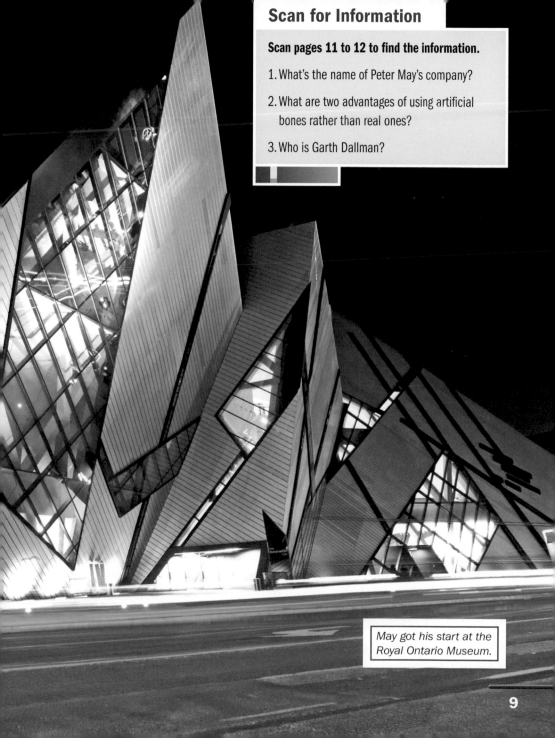

Scan for Information

Scan pages 11 to 12 to find the information.

1. What's the name of Peter May's company?

2. What are two advantages of using artificial bones rather than real ones?

3. Who is Garth Dallman?

May got his start at the Royal Ontario Museum.

It's rare for May's company, Research Casting International, or RCI, to mount actual dinosaur bones. Most of their work involves making casts of the real bones in order to create artificial ones. The basic process begins with painting the actual bone with a coat of rubber to recreate the look, feel, and shape of a real dinosaur bone. Next, the workers wrap the cast shape in a hard covering to support it. Lastly, they mix the fiberglass compound and pour it into the shape of the bone. The fiberglass displaces the air in the center of the cast shape and when it dries, the finished product is an artificial bone that is identical in shape to the real one.

There are a number of advantages to using artificial bones when creating model skeletons for museum displays. These artificial bones are cheaper and lighter than the actual bones, which is advantageous to both parties involved in the process. It's an advantage to the museum in that it helps keep costs down and budgets under control. It's also helpful to the dinosaur builders because the reduced weight makes the bones easier to work with and the skeletons easier to mount for display. Another benefit of using artificial bones is the fact that holes can be drilled into them in order to mount them on the steel frameworks. This allows the skeletons to be assembled on central supporting structures, thus making them more stable. In addition, paleontologists obviously prefer not to drill holes in the actual ancient bones as the drilling would damage them, thereby compromising an important link to our planet's past.

The work done by RCI is complicated and incredibly detailed, requiring great accuracy on the part of the dinosaur builders. Most of the skeletons being recreated are incomplete, which forces the builders to shape the missing parts themselves in order to recreate the skeletal components of an animal that has been extinct for millions of years. They accomplish this by using technical drawings of fossils and of the dinosaurs themselves as guides. It's the type of work in which it's critical to be accurate and the craftsmen and women can't deviate from the plans; they are tightly restricted to scientific reality. Unfortunately, there isn't exactly a 'Dinosaur Building Academy' or even many written guidelines or publications about how to mount dinosaurs. Therefore, with each display they construct May's team must learn on the job.

Some of May's team members have no background experience related specifically to dinosaur making or even to science. A few even started their careers in completely different positions. One member, Garth Dallman, is a **blacksmith**[6] by trade. He explains that the skills he learned as a blacksmith have proved to be extremely relevant in reconstructing dinosaurs. Unfortunately, they're also skills that are not often useful in the outside business world anymore. Dallman explains: "[Being a dinosaur builder] is a good **blend**[7] of science and art. My skills are actually … I guess they're coming back in a lot of ways. Some people [want] decorative iron working, but the actual trade of blacksmithing is a bit of a dinosaur too."

---

[6]**blacksmith:** a skilled worker who makes and fixes things made of iron
[7]**blend:** combination; a mixture of two or more things

Putting a dinosaur skeleton together is a natural version of a construction project, but one in which everything must fit together like a giant **jigsaw puzzle**.[8] The unfortunate aspect of this puzzle is that if just one piece of the skeleton is placed incorrectly, the entire structure could be thrown off. Kevin Prudek's job is to actually put the huge reptiles' skeletons together. He explains: "If you don't start with the leg in the right way, then the hip will be wrong and the backbone will be wrong. So you really have to know what you're doing from the beginning on so that everything works properly. I mean, it's like a puzzle. You can't put one piece in wrong and expect everything else to fit."

---

[8]**jigsaw puzzle:** a form of entertainment in which a picture on paper or wood that has been cut into pieces is put back together

Infer Meaning

1. On page 12, what does Garth Dallman mean when he says "the actual trade of blacksmithing is a bit of a dinosaur too"? Write a definition for the slang meaning of the word 'dinosaur.'

2. On page 14, what does the writer imply with 'a natural version of a construction project'? Write an explanation of the phrase.

Pigeon

Archaeopteryx

Ornitholestes

The builders in May's workshop do much more than just build dinosaurs, however. They also help scientists solve the mysteries and **controversies**[9] surrounding these ancient creatures' appearance and behavior. Since they roamed the earth long before humans did, there is no human record of them, and scientists can often only hypothesize as to the reality of the lives and actions of these giant beasts. Kevin Seymour explains just how crucial the quality and accuracy of mounting is to science. "[The dinosaur builders] are **in the fore[front]**[10] of the controversies of how these animals lived and acted," he says, "because how you put them together, what kind of **posture**[11] you put them in, really is the way they're interpreted. A paleontologist might say 'we believe it's done this way', and the guy who's mounting it could say, 'I don't think the bones go together that way. Look.' You know? So there is this conversation back and forth that's quite valuable."

Seymour goes on to explain that the positioning, or 'posing,' of the dinosaurs when on display can place the mount on the level of art. It's important that the body is mounted correctly and looks natural as opposed to looking strange or out of proportion due to poor positioning. Seymour explains: "There's a very big difference between an average mount and a fantastic mount. A really beautifully posed mount is a work of art." The level of respect received for a job well done seems to justify the amount of work needed to recreate the figure of one of these huge, ancient creatures.

---

[9]**controversy:** public disagreement, usually involving strong opinions and an important subject
[10]**in the forefront:** in the most important or noticeable position
[11]**posture:** the position in which the body is held by a person or animal

In addition to helping dinosaur displays to be considered art, the dinosaur builders are also the public face of paleontology. They deal with the results, or the 'big show,' that follows all of the difficult work done by paleontologists. They're the ones who discover and document the fossils and bones that tell us so much about the dinosaurs. The dinosaur builders are the ones who bring that history to life with their recreations of animals that have not walked the earth for millions of years.

Peter May describes what it's like to be involved in the work of constructing and mounting these ancient beasts. "It's like anything. It becomes a **labor of love**,"[12] he declares. "These guys were **king of the hill**[13] back then, you know? As you work on it, **your mind drifts**[14] and then when it's mounted, it's on display in a museum, one skeleton becomes a part of the whole, which is the history of our world." It's obvious that educating people about the animals that once dominated all others is something that this dinosaur builder both loves and respects.

---

[12]**labor of love:** *(expression)* a piece of work done for one's own pleasure or to please someone else, and not for money or other gain
[13]**king of the hill:** *(expression)* the most important or powerful
[14]**(one's) mind drifts:** the mind or thoughts go in unexpected or unplanned directions

After You Read

1. What is the purpose of paragraph 1 on page 4?
   A. to introduce the topic of dinosaur building
   B. to explain the implicit connection between people and dinosaurs
   C. to share details about the skeletons of dinosaurs
   D. to contrast the different types of dinosaurs in museums

2. From the information in paragraph 1 on page 7, it can be inferred that Peter May:
   A. is too busy to finish all his work
   B. needs to hire more employees
   C. has a busy, successful business
   D. gets complaints about noise from his neighbors

3. On page 7, the stegosaurus skeleton is given as an example of how:
   A. slowly Peter May must work
   B. Peter May views the complexity of his work
   C. Peter May exploits dinosaurs
   D. Peter May began his career

4. Which of the following summarizes how Peter May became a dinosaur builder?
   A. It was a goal he pursued from a young age.
   B. He chose the career immediately after he graduated high school.
   C. He took advantage of an opportunity to work with several different museums.
   D. He wanted to find the best way to make the most money.

5. Which of the following is NOT an advantage of using an artificial bone?
   A. size
   B. cost
   C. weight
   D. preservation

6. The word 'accuracy' in paragraph 1 on page 12 can be replaced by:
   A. tension
   B. convergence
   C. struggle
   D. precision